RUNNING MEETINGS

Other books in the Penguin Pocket Series

THE AUSTRALIAN CALORIE COUNTER
THE AUSTRALIAN EASY SPELLER
AUSTRALIAN GARDENING CALENDAR
BEST EVER IDEAS FOR CHILDREN'S PARTIES
CASSEROLES FOR FAMILY AND FRIENDS
CHESS MADE EASY
CHOOSING A NAME FOR YOUR BABY
CHOOSING AUSTRALIAN WINES
THE COMPACT GUIDE TO WRITING LETTERS
FAMILY FIRST AID
GABRIEL GATÉ'S FAST PASTA
GABRIEL GATÉ'S FAVOURITE FAST RECIPES
GABRIEL GATÉ'S ONE-DISH DINNERS
GOOD FOOD FOR BABIES AND TODDLERS
HOW TO MAKE OVER 200 COCKTAILS
HOW TO PLAY MAH JONG
JULIE STAFFORD'S JUICING BOOK
MICROWAVE MEALS IN MINUTES
MICROWAVE TIPS AND TECHNIQUES
PLAYING CASINO GAMES TO WIN
THE POCKET AUSSIE FACT BOOK
REMOVING STAINS
SPEAKING IN PUBLIC
TRAINING YOUR MEMORY
USING YOUR NOODLES
WEDDING ETIQUETTE
YOUR NEW BABY

CHAIRING ~~and~~ RUNNING MEETINGS

Nina Valentine

PENGUIN BOOKS

Penguin Books Australia Ltd
487 Maroondah Highway, PO Box 257
Ringwood, Victoria 3134, Australia
Penguin Books Ltd
Harmondsworth, Middlesex, England
Viking Penguin, A Division of Penguin Books USA Inc.
375 Hudson Street, New York, New York 10014, USA
Penguin Books Canada Limited
10 Alcorn Avenue, Toronto, Ontario, Canada M4V 3B2
Penguin Books (N.Z.) Ltd
Cnr Rosedale and Airborne Roads, Albany, Auckland, New Zealand

First published by Penguin Books Australia Ltd 1993
This revised edition published 1996

10 9 8 7 6 5 4 3 2

Copyright © Nina Valentine, 1993

All rights reserved. Without limiting the rights under copyright reserved above, no part of this publication may be reproduced, stored in or introduced into a retrieval system, or transmitted, in any form or by any means (electronic, mechanical, photocopying, recording or otherwise), without the prior written permission of both the copyright owner and the above publisher of this book.

Illustrations by Steve Panozzo
Cover photograph by Phil Thomas
Typeset in Cheltenham Book Condensed
Printed by Australian Print Group, Maryborough, Victoria

National Library of Australia
Cataloguing-in-Publication data

Valentine, Nina.
 Chairing and running meetings.

 Rev. ed.
 Includes index.
 ISBN 0 14 025763 2.

 1. Meetings. 2. Public speaking. I. Title. (Series: Penguin pocket series).

658.456

CONTENTS

INTRODUCTION / vii

1 IN THE CHAIR / 1

2 THE SECRETARY / 15

3 THE TREASURER / 27

4 THE CONDUCT OF A MEETING / 35

5 THE ANNUAL MEETING / 49

6 SPEAKING IN PUBLIC / 59

7 ANSWERS TO YOUR QUESTIONS / 79

APPENDICES / 101
1   Guidelines for a simple constitution / 101
2   The rules of debate / 105
3   Rules and effects relating to formal motions / 107

GLOSSARY / 112

INDEX / 115

INTRODUCTION

Many books about meeting procedure are more learned than this one. Usually you will find that they are designed for parliamentary debate, or for council proceedings; seldom if ever is there a book designed specifically for ordinary people in small groups or service clubs – Scouts, CWA, Zonta, Apex, Lions, Rotary, church societies, sporting bodies, school associations – working to help the community.

I hope this book will fill the gap.

When you are asked to stand for an executive position in your club, that is, president, chairperson, secretary or treasurer, try not to say immediately 'No thank you – I couldn't do that'. Try to think instead in a positive manner. Given a little help, everyone is capable of running a meeting, writing minutes or paying accounts. This book is that 'little help' you may need to be a good executive.

No one likes to go to meetings that become top-heavy with business, that drag on beyond the allotted time and achieve little – or nothing. Floor members must know procedures too, so that they can help the meeting to progress smoothly and, if necessary, help to control the executive. A meeting of efficient executives and knowledgeable floor members will be enjoyable. It is also with this in mind that this book has been written.

The chapters on meeting procedures and public speaking have been kept simple because they are designed to make things easy for executive and membership alike. You will find explanations of more advanced meeting procedures in Chapter 7, useful supplementary material in the Appendices, and definitions of a number of terms in the Glossary.

If you follow the streamlining techniques outlined in this book your meetings will be a great deal more fun. There will be little boredom. There will be willing workers on your committees. There will be happy faces around any meeting table, and members in roles they never thought possible before. You will have a good, lively, expanding membership that welcomes challenges and commitment. And *that* makes for happy meetings.

A NOTE ABOUT TERMS AND TITLES

Throughout the book I have used 'chairperson' as the descriptive term for the person who takes the chair at meetings; however, in giving examples of meeting procedure I have alternated two correct forms of address – 'Madam Chairman' and 'Mr Chairman'. This acknowledges that while 'chairperson' is desirable as a non-sexist descriptive term it is not considered correct to use it in forms of address ('Madam Chairperson' or 'Mr Chairperson'). At the same time it is understood that an organisation or a holder of the office may prefer a particular term (for example 'Chairman'), either as a description or as a form of address.

It is so usual for the president of an organisation to act as chairperson that the terms 'president' and 'chairperson' are often taken to mean the same thing. This book makes a distinction between them because in some organisations the president does not chair meetings. The term 'president' is therefore used only to refer to the spokesperson for an organisation. 'Vice-president' is used in a different way, to describe the role of assistant to the chairperson.

1 IN THE CHAIR

To be a good chairperson you need not be a genius – though there will be times when you feel this would indeed be an asset!

There are, of course, other more attainable assets. You'll need to believe in the ultimate purpose of your club, be interested in the members of the group, give time to thinking about the purpose and the planning of your meetings – and you'll need to learn business procedures.

You'll need, above all that, tact, impartiality, enthusiasm, efficiency, a sense of responsibility and a sense of humour.

As well, especially if you are president as well as chairperson, you'll need a good sense of public relations, because to outsiders you *are* the club (see 'A note about terms and titles'). This comes about because the duties of a president include the playing of host to visitors and the representation of the club on public occasions. In making public statements the spokesperson must be sure that she or he expresses the policies of the club, and not private opinions.

IMPORTANCE OF THE OFFICE

More than any other member of the executive the chairperson can make or break a group.

The next time you have been to a meeting you think was poorly run, think back to what happened. Was it the fault of the person in the chair? Most times it is. Conversely, the next time you have been to an efficient, interesting meeting, think back over the procedures. Yes, the person in the chair was good at the job, and controlled events. Because of this the business was transacted in a calm, decisive manner, and the will of the majority was ascertained.

If the chairperson is easy to approach, easy to talk to, encouraging to members, and definite in opinions and decision-making, the club is fortunate. Pity the organisation with a chairperson who shirks responsibility and who plays favourites!

If the chairperson is able to convey to each member of each committee just what the club is aiming to do, and authority is delegated where necessary, she or he is fulfilling that role admirably.

WHAT DO I DO?

No one is born with a chairperson's skills, but some people have characteristics or qualities that make it easier for them. The characteristics may be innate but the knowing what to do, and when to do it, comes from basic principles that can be learnt. To fulfil your function well should be your ultimate aim, and to this end there are certain things you'll need to do now that you are in the chair.

Be in touch

First, make yourself familiar with the **constitution** of your club (see box) and have it with you at all meetings so that you can refer to it if a contentious point arises.

The aims of a club as set out in the constitution are a byword for a good chairperson, which is a good reason for making yourself conversant with this document before the first meeting you conduct.

YOUR CONSTITUTION

A constitution is a flexible document designed to cover the needs and aims of any particular group, club or committee. It should be seen as an adaptable master plan for the efficient running of your organisation.

The important thing to remember is that every group, however small, needs a constitution if the group is to work properly. Any disagreement or argument is easier to solve if you have rules to work from – *and* the rules are written down in the constitution.

A constitution may cover matters of membership, including:

- types of membership
- conditions of membership – for example that a member automatically loses the right to membership if three consecutive meetings are missed without an apology
- whether Life Memberships are given for outstanding service to the group.

Remember, always, that an alteration to your constitution is usually of major importance and must be handled carefully, with due regard for the time it takes to send, *in writing*, notice of that change to every member of the club.

A constitution may have any number of clauses, depending on the type of organisation. The format given in Appendix 1 is for a very simple constitution, and may be altered to suit your particular group, club or committee.

As far as possible, look over the **minute books** of previous years. They will give you an overall picture of the aims of your club and will refresh your memory of fund-raising functions and other events.

Make sure you know the names of your members, and refer to them by name whenever possible. Try to draw out the shy members of your group. They often have great potential, needing only a little tactful encouragement from you to give their best. Remember that the future of your club rests with the membership, and try to develop all their talents, taking a long-term view.

Encourage your members to learn about the conduct of meetings: this expertise is not just for executives. Knowledge of procedure among members leads to better meetings, less time taken, and greater satisfaction.

Try also to increase the membership by getting to know who might be interested in your objectives and inviting them to come to special meetings.

Organise and delegate

Ability to organise is essential, because as chairperson you have to plan so much ahead. You must ascertain that all office-bearers are aware of their separate duties; plan the programme for the year; plan regular meetings; communicate with your various committees; and delegate authority.

In particular, know *when* to delegate. Give certain duties to your **vice-president** (some constitutions call for *two* assistants, a senior vice-president and a junior vice-president) because in this way you ensure that the club has a competent substitute to chair the meetings if you are absent; and, in all probability, you are training a good chairperson for the future.

Be confident

Usually the chairperson conducts all meetings, though in some clubs members take the chair in rotation so that each member learns how to control a meeting. Whatever the case, the chairperson needs to be familiar with the elements of the office and with meeting procedures.

Among the qualities for a good chairperson, confidence is primary. Armed with your knowledge of good planning and of how to conduct an efficient meeting, you can be sure that you will have the confidence to handle events and to keep order with tact and consideration.

Be patient, keep your temper, think quickly, and be firm yet friendly in your manner from the chair. You will need to be objective in your thinking, for you must be impartial in all your decisions: a biased chairperson is of no use to any organisation, however large or small.

PREPARING FOR A MEETING

An efficient chairperson runs the meeting from an **agenda** prepared beforehand, sometimes with the help of the secretary.

Having a clearly set out agenda covering all matters relevant to that particular meeting will give you confidence and enable you to feel that *you* are in charge of the meeting – not vice versa. Treat your agenda as a set of rules or a recipe for a good meeting (see boxed example on page 8).

Any questions asked prior to the meeting must be brought forward for discussion. This can be done if you contact your other office-bearers before you meet, and plan the agenda to include those matters.

It is most useful to have a list of names, addresses and phone numbers in a special club notebook: this makes your preparation much easier.

8 Chairing and Running Meetings

AGENDA

1. Chairperson declares the meeting open.
2. Guests are welcomed by the chairperson.
3. Apologies.
4. Minutes of the previous meeting.
5. Business arising from the minutes.
6. Correspondence.
7. Reports.
8. General business:
    Adjourned business.
    Notice of motion.
    List of matters to be discussed: rose garden; recycling; fundraising; Christmas function.
    Further business.
9. Date, time and place of next meeting.
10. Close of meeting.

All **correspondence** must be read before the meeting, so that no communication, request or invitation comes as a surprise.

The **minutes** must also be examined before the meeting so that matters arising from them can be noted for further discussion with the membership.

AT THE MEETING

Be punctual. Commencing meetings on time gives a decisive feeling from the chair and also means that the meeting will conclude at a reasonable hour.

Once you have begun proceedings you must stay put: the chairperson does not leave the chair during an ordinary meeting.

Make sure that a **quorum** is present (see box): know what your constitution says about this.

IS THERE A QUORUM?

Numbers for a quorum will vary. It is usually a quarter of the normal membership, but your constitution will state this clearly. No meeting may begin unless a quorum is present, for it would be inadvisable to pass a motion that could be seen as controversial, unless a reasonable number of members are there to discuss it and vote on it.

Next, peruse the agenda quickly for errors and omissions. With good forward planning, this approach will transmit a feeling of stability and certainty to the meeting.

Who may speak?

Every member has an equal right to speak.

An alert chairperson sees that equal opportunities are given to all present, and that discussions are kept to the point of the **motion**. Try to curb over-enthusiastic members, but do it with the utmost tact: the enthusiasm that is threatening to overwhelm the meeting is often necessary to the project you are planning, and you do not wish to offend. The rule that each member may speak only once to any one motion is a most handy tool, for it may be used to quell that over-zealous speaker without any personal motive being given, or any offence taken.

Remember that remarks and motions must be addressed through the chair, not from one side of the room to the other. Until they follow it automatically members should be reminded of this rule, which is designed to stop private conversations getting out of hand and ruining the purpose of the meeting.

While a floor member is speaking it is up to the person in the chair to see that other people remain quiet. Business meetings are held for discussion of business, not for gossip sessions conducted while a member is speaking about some matter of importance to the club.

When the chairperson is called upon to give a ruling on a point of procedure or debate, it needs to be done promptly, with the reasons given for the ruling.

Motions

A chairperson may not move a motion, though it is permissible to make a suggestion and ask for a motion that picks up or expands that idea. This of course demonstrates that the chairperson is impartial in the conduct of the meeting. The chairperson directs the discussion, taking alternate speakers **for** and **against** the motion, but this is a very different matter from expressing personal opinions and perhaps unduly swaying the meeting.

So remember that you need a **mover** of a motion, and a **seconder**, *before* any discussion takes place. At too many meetings it is the reverse; then you have loads of discussion, followed by a motion, then the same discussion all over again, before the vote is taken. A great waste of time!

Only after remarks, opinions and arguments have been heard is the motion **put to the vote**. When discussion becomes repetitive, give the mover the **right of reply** and then put the motion immediately, thus avoiding unnecessary delays.

Of course while one motion is being considered, no other motion or irrelevant matter may be introduced (see 'Amendments' in Chapter 4). It is up to the person in the chair to recognise that another idea is being introduced that has little or no bearing upon the matter in hand. It is also up to the chairperson to quash this irrelevancy.

Voting

Upon calling for the vote to be taken, the chairperson should nominate the method to be used, for example: 'Ladies and gentlemen, it has been moved by Mrs Jones, seconded by Mr Nguyen, that we have a party. All those in favour please raise their right hands'. Or you may nominate the more traditional method, especially if your club is accustomed to it: 'Those in favour, say aye'. In each case you must call for the negative vote by saying 'Those against please raise your hands' or 'Those against, say nay'. Use one voting method consistently during your term of office.

If you have only one dissenting member that member has the right to register a vote also. It is quite correct for dissenting members to ask for the **dissent** to carry their names against it. The chairperson accepts the request and makes sure that the secretary notes the names of the dissenters against the motion. Finally, at the end of the voting time you say 'The motion is carried' or 'The motion is lost'.

THE CASTING VOTE

Usually the chairperson has the **casting vote** when votes are **deadlocked** (equal numbers voting for and against). When this happens the chairperson votes against the motion, thus retaining the **status quo**. If the chair were to vote the other way, the decision for change would have been directed by one person.

The status quo ('what exists now') is always upheld, to demonstrate the chairperson's impartiality.

Dissent from a ruling

Should there be a dissent from the chairperson's ruling – about any matter – accept it with good grace. Whether the dissent is upheld or not does not really matter. What does matter is that if the chairperson takes this action as impersonal and objective, she or he will earn the respect of the membership and in this way bring stature to the office.

YOUR AIM

You are directing the meeting; the meeting is not directing you. Give a good example to your members, as this is the best teacher and will ensure good chairing in the foreseeable future.

A BALANCING ACT

Chairpersons have been known to take over meetings rather than simply to direct them. This is quite wrong, yet it happens frequently. The chairperson has to determine the will of the majority in any matter before the chair and see that it is carried out; at club level this is the difference between dictatorship and democracy. Achieving the right balance depends largely on a fundamental knowledge of meeting procedures.

Your professionalism will reflect well on the whole organisation – you can then permit yourself a little quiet pride in the work you are doing and in the office you hold. Such pride will usually give you the satisfaction of seeing your membership increase in both numbers and enthusiasm. Good chairing skills (see page 14), more than anything else, makes for good clubs. What an aim!

With that goes your impartiality, which ensures that the will of the majority *is* carried out. That really does make for excellent relationships within any group of people – female or male, old or young, small or large, in the country or in the city.

14 Chairing and Running Meetings

QUALITIES OF A GOOD CHAIRPERSON

Impartiality
Knowledge of procedures
Confidence
Enthusiasm
Tact
Efficiency
Good organisational skills
Sense of responsibility
Ability to delegate
Leadership
Friendliness
Sense of pride
Readiness to cooperate

2 THE SECRETARY

A secretary's job is not an easy one, particularly in a large organisation, but it can be happy and rewarding.

A good secretary needs organising ability, a pleasing, easy-to-get-on-with personality, the ability to work hard; and time, patience and tact! A large order? It's not an impossible order to fill, for although they may sometimes long for divine assistance, most secretaries have all the necessary qualities without being aware of them.

DUTIES

As a secretary you must understand certain basic duties and carry them out efficiently.

Your first duties are to book the hall or room for the regular meetings and to send notices (if necessary) to all members of the club.

As other members of the executive must do, you attend all general meetings and the meetings of the committees and subcommittees to which you have been appointed. You must deal with all correspondence for your club, and keep a register of its members. You check the accounts before handing them on to the treasurer. In most organisations the secretary is one of the people authorised to sign cheques used for payment of accounts, so make sure that your signature is registered with the appropriate bank or building society.

You must keep in constant touch with the chairperson, and relieve that busy person of small tasks as they come to hand. You must also send out notices of **special meetings** and make sure that any changes are well advertised. At election time you deal with nomination forms.

Before meetings you should, if appropriate, send out a copy of the previous meeting's minutes to the members and help the chairperson plan the agenda.

AT THE MEETING

You arrive on time for the meeting (making sure that you have a copy of the minutes with you), check to see if a quorum is present, and advise the chairperson if necessary.

Apologies

As the meeting proceeds you must record the apologies, and either count the number of members present or note their names. Names are preferred, for it is then possible to check who has attended meetings and who has not.

Reading the minutes

At the appropriate stage of the agenda your task is to read the minutes of the previous meeting. Stand up, and hold the minutes up in front of you or put them on a lectern. Use your finger as a pointer so that you can mark your place on the page when you look at your audience. Read clearly, with due emphasis and intelligence, so that everyone is aware of what really did take place at the last meeting. It also adds to the interest of the meeting if the minutes are read well.

After the minutes have been confirmed, hand them to the chairperson for signature.

Correspondence

Part of a secretary's responsibility is to bring all 'inwards' and 'outwards' correspondence before each meeting. Make this a practice from now on: many clubs never see copies of the outgoing correspondence, and so have no idea of the worth of their secretary as a letter-writer. Unless copies of these letters are tabled, there is no way of knowing if the will of the meeting has been carried out correctly.

Secretaries need to be able to express themselves well on paper. The impression made by any letter of a secretary is most important, because it is a showcase for the rest of the membership. Poorly written letters may give the impression of a poorly educated club that would have little chance of being a force in the community. This is not necessarily true, of course, but it is, unfortunately, the perception when correspondence is not considered up to the mark. For secretaries themselves, bringing all correspondence before a meeting provides a useful check on the appropriateness of their letters.

In a large club where there is much correspondence, sort the letters into categories or place them in labelled folders, to make it easier for yourself and the floor members to follow. The categories might be 'Matters dealt with', 'Current events', and 'Future matters' – but devise your own to suit the needs of your organisation.

Taking the minutes

Your minutes are seen as a correct report of what took place at a particular meeting. Take your notes very carefully during meetings and perhaps enlist the aid of a small, unobtrusive tape recorder to which you may refer when writing up your notes after meetings. When you play the tape back in private you will be surprised, often shocked and frequently amused by what was actually said.

Make notes about any reports that have been particularly interesting and write down the exact wording of all motions, **amendments** and **resolutions**, making sure also that you record whether they were lost or carried.

Record all motions that have been discussed, although it is correct to leave out the detail of those that have been withdrawn. This withdrawing of a motion before it's voted on may be done only with the consent of both the mover and the seconder and a unanimous vote from the floor.

During meetings you will be asked to read out the wording of a motion once it is under discussion, to be certain that each member knows exactly what is being argued. Your role is to be accurate in your recording of the motion and careful in your reading of it.

AFTER THE MEETING

Write up your minutes as soon as you can (see boxed example). Matters are then fresh in your mind and it is much easier to express yourself clearly because of this. Remember also that tape recorders have been known to fail or that part of the tape may be unintelligible.

There should be no erasures in your writing of the minutes. If you do find an error, rule it out, make the alteration and have the chairperson initial it. This is simply a device to prevent anyone tampering with the minutes and getting away with it. It may seem a little pedantic for a small membership, but it is as well to do things correctly at all levels, for good habits die hard.

MINUTES

MINUTES OF THE MEETING OF THE GLEE CLUB OF WHOOPEE, HELD ON TUESDAY MAY 4 1993, IN PARADISE HALL, AT 8 P.M.

The chairperson declared the meeting open at 8.05 p.m.

PRESENT Jean Singer, Henry Warbler, Peter Bass, Florence Nightingale, Joan Larkin, John Sang, Coralee Timbre, William Trill, Jonathan Beat, Joanne Clef, Adam Note, Jess Pitch and Lorna Broadcast.

APOLOGIES Joan Sunderland, Nathan Summers, Paolo Domingo and Jane Carden. The apologies were accepted on the motion of Jean Singer, seconded by Coralee Timbre. <u>Carried</u>.

MINUTES The minutes of the last meeting were read by the secretary, confirmed on the motion of Joanne Clef and seconded by Jess Pitch. <u>Carried</u>.

BUSINESS ARISING The secretary reported that she had written to the Shire Choir to ask them to amalgamate with the Whoopee Glee Club. No reply has yet been received.

continued on next page

continued from previous page

CORRESPONDENCE Three letters were received: an invitation from the Sydney Opera House Choral Committee, for the Glee Club to sing in the September Festival in Sydney; a letter from past member, Andrew Tenor, to thank the club for its letter of condolence; and a publicity brochure from the Royal South Street Competitions, Ballarat, outlining next year's Choral Eisteddfod.

A show of hands received the correspondence by general consent.

TREASURER'S REPORT The Financial Statement showed a balance of $200.80. Moved by the treasurer that this statement be received, and that an account for $45.00 for music be passed for payment. Seconded by Joan Larkin. <u>Carried</u>.

OTHER REPORTS The social committee outlined its plan for the Glee Club's Reunion to be held in March 1994.

The fundraising committee's report gave the current economic climate as the reason for little support shown for the last raffle held by the club.

The music-selection committee explained the reasons for changing from traditional music to modern ballads.

The subcommittee appointed to look into the matter of a history of the Glee Club being written stated that it had two problems: the high cost of printing, and the difficulty of finding a suitable writer.

Moved on the motion of Florence Nightingale that reports be received; seconded by John Sang. <u>Carried</u>.

GENERAL BUSINESS   No adjourned business.

Moved by Peter Bass that we take part in the September Festival in Sydney; seconded by Lorna Broadcast. After much discussion as to the costs of such a journey and the time involved, <u>the motion was carried</u>. Henry Warbler asked that his name be recorded as a negative vote because he thought the commitment was too great for such a small group.

Moved by Jess Pitch, seconded by Adam Note, that we take part in the Royal South Street Competitions in September 1994. Because of the distance to be travelled and the high cost of accommodation, <u>the motion was lost</u>.

Moved by William Trill, seconded by Joanne Clef, that Nina Valentine be asked to write the history of the Whoopee Glee Club. <u>Carried unanimously</u>.

Jonathan Beat offered the club his collection of sheet music, gathered over the past forty years. Moved by Coralee Timbre, seconded by Peter Bass, that this magnificent gift be accepted with appreciation. <u>Carried unanimously</u>.

Moved by Henry Warbler, seconded by Adam Note, that we hold a fete in Paradise Hall on September 25 1993 to raise funds for publishing the history of the

continued on next page

24 Chairing and Running Meetings

> *continued from previous page*
>
> Whoopee Glee Club. Both members thought the fete would raise enough to pay the author's fee and the cost of printing, since the Glee Club has many art and craft people in its ranks and among its friends.
>
> An amendment was moved by Jean Singer, seconded by William Trill, that the fete be held on October 9 1993. They both thought another two weeks would give members more time to prepare and that the weather would be better for outside stalls. Carried.
>
> The president then put the motion <u>that we</u> hold a fete in Paradise Hall on October 9 1993 to raise funds for publishing the history of the Whoopee Glee Club. <u>Carried unanimously</u>.
>
> NOTICE OF MOTION Florence Nightingale moved that the annual subscription to the Glee Club of Whoopee be raised to $20.00.
>
> NEXT MEETING To be held on Tuesday May 18 1993, in Paradise Hall at 8 p.m.
>
> There being no further business the meeting closed at 10 p.m.

Follow-up

When you've written the minutes, go over them and note where action is needed. Deal promptly with the matters that have been left to your care – they may take longer than you think. Write any letters necessary to carry out the will of the group and, well before the date set down for the next meeting, follow up any matters pertaining to your organisation.

ORGANISING A GUEST SPEAKER

It is customary for the secretary to make all the arrangements for a guest speaker. It is a good idea to phone, but also to set down the arrangements in a letter. Make sure that everything is done for the comfort and convenience of the speaker and that all the details are understood by you, the club, and the speaker.

Well in advance, arrange the following:

- precise details of venue and time of arrival
- travel arrangements and accommodation
- whether the speaker is to be paid a fee
- how long the address is to be
- permission for questions to be put after the address.

Closer to the time, phone the speaker and run through all the arrangements again. This is important, as the passing of time can blur the details.

Remember that the best arrival time may be well after the beginning of the meeting, as it can be embarrassing for a guest speaker to sit through business before giving a speech. It's also time-wasting for the speaker – most are busy people who can ill afford to waste even fifteen minutes.

DO IT NOW!

There are many duties an efficient secretary can undertake. Often secretaries are so efficient that they look for more areas in which they can be of service, making this a most rewarding position to fill. If you make your motto 'Do it now', the task will be lots easier. Added to that, your service and your enthusiasm will benefit your club (and you) enormously.

QUALITIES OF A GOOD SECRETARY

Capacity for work
Initiative
Organising ability
Meticulous attention to detail
Tact
Ability to write well
Cooperation with others
Easy, open personality

3 THE TREASURER

Some people who belong to clubs are guilty of thinking that the treasurer's position is a minor one in the executive structure. This is far from the truth. Ask anyone at all who has had something to do with an association whose treasurer has been less than diligent – or downright dishonest – and you will have this thought banished from your mind for ever.

Most clubs have some fundraising activites, and all of them have dues – however small – to be collected, cared for, and perhaps invested. All these tasks come within the scope of the treasurer.

To be a good treasurer you must be careful, methodical and strictly honest. Your members must know that they can trust you with their funds. A knowledge of bookkeeping or accounting is a decided asset though it is not a necessity, particularly in smaller groups. As well as matters pertaining to money, there are certain general duties you'll carry out in the position of treasurer.

DUTIES

As treasurer you are responsible for all the financial dealings of your organisation. You must attend all meetings to watch the finances and to advise on financial matters. You must make out all receipts, and bank all money, *without deductions*. Make sure you have a list of members and mark them off as they pay their subscriptions.

Keep all pay-in slips: this is most important as it is easy to fall into the trap of paying a small account from cash in hand, forgetting that you did it, and then finding the books won't balance. Obtain bank statements regularly, and make sure they tally with your own records.

Make no payments without the correct authority. It is usual to have cheques signed by the treasurer and two members of the executive. Withdrawals should be made only when two with authority have signed the necessary forms.

Keep (and balance!) the **petty cash**. The amount should be decided by the executive and should be kept to a minimum. If day-to-day expenses (for example postage) go up, request an increase.

Keep your bookkeeping record in a clear, simple way. Pay by cheque: this is an easy way to create a record. Write down everything systematically in a book (if it's a large organisation use a ledger). File *all* relevant documents, including receipts, vouchers, petty cash withdrawals and bank statements.

Once a year or at such other times as the constitution requires, there will be an **audit** of your books. Help the auditors in every way you can: they are, after all (if the audit is completed successfully) giving proof to your membership that you have been doing a good, honest job.

Watch the finances of your club carefully, and never be afraid to offer suggestions to your chairperson or secretary. Often the best chairperson is hopeless when it comes to managing money matters, and you are there to guide and advise.

Before each meeting prepare a **financial statement** (see boxed example; also called a **financial report** or **balance sheet**). If the statement is long or complicated it should be sent out to members so that they can study it before the meeting.

FINANCIAL STATEMENT

PARENTS AND FRIENDS ASSOCIATION

STATEMENT OF RECEIPTS AND PAYMENTS FOR THE MONTH OF JUNE, 1993

RECEIPTS		PAYMENTS	
Balance brought forward	$124	Hire of hall	$80
Subscriptions	$80	Cost of music	$100
Donation	$10	Drinks	$44
Proceeds from weekly dances	$356	Prizes	$18
Sale of raffle tickets	$228	Printing of tickets	$16
Sale of drinks at dances	$54	Decorations	$26
		Balance (surplus of receipts over payments)	$568
	$852		$852

AT THE MEETING

What do you do at the meeting itself?

First you **present accounts for payment**. Then you make certain that this list of accounts is the subject of a motion, and is passed for payment. Have your chairperson initial them as proof that this motion was carried.

Your next task is to read **the financial statement**. Read it clearly, adding explanations of anything that is not obvious, to help those who do not readily understand figures. Be prepared to answer questions.

When that is concluded you **move the appropriate motion** by saying, 'I move that this financial statement be received, and that the current accounts are passed for payment'. This means that only a seconder has to be called for, thus moving the meeting along more quickly.

Do assist all you can in the running of a successful meeting. A treasurer can be a fine example of a good, alert member.

AFTER THE MEETING

After the meeting is over, draw cheques and pay all the accounts that met the approval of the membership. Be absolutely sure that you obtain a receipt for each payment: you are caring for money that belongs to other people, and you must be *seen* to be doing just that. It is worth repeating that the best way is to pay everything by cheque, as your cheque butts are the best and easiest record of the club's expenditure.

BE AWARE

You are the watchdog of your organisation, and as such you should be up to the minute with all financial matters necessary to its well-being. As treasurer and a member of the executive you should do everything possible to forward the interests of your club and then look to do more, especially in fundraising activities. The more money you can report having handled since the last meeting the more inner satisfaction you will know.

It is not unknown for treasurers to abscond with the funds, or for incompetent treasurers to tie themselves into financial knots. It is not unknown for treasurers who are not meticulous in their record-keeping to muddle club funds and their own money. All clubs should be aware of these dangers and should elect a responsible person to this vital position.

If clubs follow the simple rules laid down in this book the treasurer's work is much easier. It won't keep the dishonest from being dishonest or the muddler from being a muddler; but if club members select their executive with care and thought, the danger of choosing the wrong person for treasurer is greatly reduced.

QUALITIES OF A GOOD TREASURER

Honesty
Trustworthiness
Bookkeeping ability
Care
Methodical habits
Sense of responsibility

4 THE CONDUCT OF A MEETING

Let's move on to basic meeting procedures.

You have an objective chairperson, an efficient secretary, and an honest treasurer. What more can you ask for? You can ask for well-informed floor members, who know just how a meeting should proceed.

So with this ideal executive sitting before their alert membership, all armed with agendas, the meeting will proceed – ideally – as follows.

FIRST MOVE

The secretary checks that a quorum is present, and informs the chairperson. If there's a quorum, the chairperson declares the meeting open and welcomes members and guests.

APOLOGIES

The chairperson asks, 'Are there any apologies?'. These names are taken down by the secretary to be recorded in the minutes.

Apologies must be genuine expressions of regret for non-attendance. No floor member should take a quick look about the room and lodge an apology in the name of someone not present: the apology must be made with the person's consent. Some constitutions

38 Chairing and Running Meetings

state that if a member misses three consecutive meetings without registering an apology that member is automatically deemed no longer to belong to that assocation. If haphazard apologies are accepted this makes nonsense of a rule enshrined (for very good reasons) in the constitution.

When the names of the members who have sent apologies have been recorded the chairperson asks for a mover and a seconder for acceptance of the apologies. Or, the chairperson may say, 'Is it your wish that these apologies be received by general consent?'. If this second method of accepting apologies is used, the minutes should say so.

MODES OF ADDRESS

At formal meetings members are usually addressed as 'Miss', 'Mrs', 'Ms' or 'Mr', while at informal meetings it's acceptable to address members by their given names.

In the minutes of formal meetings members' surnames are added to the mode of address ('Ms Cohen', 'Mr Chambon'), but for the minutes of informal meetings surnames should be added to given names ('Chris Morath', 'Cathy Egan').

MINUTES

The chairperson then asks the secretary to read the minutes of the previous meeting. The secretary stands, and reads the minutes clearly and with expression. There is no need to be boring just because you are reading minutes, which are often anything but boring.

The conduct of a meeting

If the minutes have been circulated before the meeting, it is assumed that all members have read them. Then the chairperson says, 'Would someone move that the minutes be taken as read?'. In either case, a mover and seconder are called for, and the minutes, upon a vote being taken, are confirmed.

If a member finds an error in the minutes it must be 'brought forward from the floor' that is, brought to the chairperson's attention. The chairperson makes the correction and initials it.

Only after that procedure is the confirmation of the minutes called for. If there is no further dissent from the matters reported in the minutes, they are now seen to be a correct record, so their confirmation is a matter of form (see also 'Voting' in Chapter 1). 'Would someone move the confirmation of the minutes? Thank you, Miss Chang. Would someone second the motion? Thank you, Mr Andersen. Those in favour? Those against? Thank you. The motion is carried.' The minutes are then signed by the chairperson.

Any member may move or second the confirmation of the minutes, whether she or he has attended the previous meeting or not, but only after any corrections have been made.

MEMORY TRIGGER

Remember correct terminology for meetings by using life situations as a trigger.

- If someone apologises, you **accept** the apology. That's the word you use at a meeting when you receive an apology.

continued on next page

> *continued from previous page*
> - When you hear something for the second time you **confirm** it in your mind. That's the word you use for the minutes, confirming them to be correct.
> - When you receive a letter in the mail you tell someone that you have **received** a communication. That's the word you use for the correspondence at a meeting. The same word is used for reports: they have been prepared, and you **receive** them.

Business arising . . .

Matters arising from the minutes are dealt with next. Small matters are tackled or commented upon immediately. Larger matters that seem likely to take up a good deal of time are **held over** until general business is called for on the agenda. The chairperson should explain this, giving the reason.

CORRESPONDENCE

The chairperson asks the secretary to read the correspondence. When this has taken place, the chairperson uses the following form. 'Would someone move that the correspondence be received? Thank you, Mrs Smith. Would someone second that motion? Thank you, Mr Suzuki. I shall put the motion to the vote. Those in favour? Those against? Thank you. Carried'.

The letters are initialled by the chairperson and discussed. Matters arising from the correspondence, if relatively unimportant, are dealt with at once, and speedily. Matters that will take more time to discuss should be held over until the general business part of the meeting.

FINANCES

The treasurer is called upon to present the financial statement. This is always the first report to be presented. It is read in a clear voice. At its conclusion the treasurer moves that this report be received. Then the chairperson asks 'Is there a seconder for the treasurer's motion?'. This is then handled like any other motion and voted upon.

As is the case with the minutes, the financial statement may be circulated before the meeting. This happens usually in larger associations where greater sums of money are involved. It enables members to read through, digest, and then to make an informed query at the meeting if they think this is necessary or if they need a point clarified.

To speed up procedures, the treasurer may also incorporate the passing of the accounts for payment into the same motion: 'Mr Chairman, I move that this report be received and that the accounts presented be passed for payment'. A seconder is called for. The vote is taken, using the same words as for an ordinary motion: 'All in favour? Anyone against? Thank you. The motion is carried'.

REPORTS

The person in the chair now calls for reports from committees or subcommittees within the group. Rather than vote on each report presented, it is more sensible and less time-wasting to receive the reports together. The reports are received after a motion, a seconder, and the approval of members. It is quite usual for the chairperson to ask, after the report has been presented, if there any questions from the floor. These are addressed through the chair to the presenter of the report and should be answered succinctly.

At the end of the reading and acceptance of all reports the meeting moves on to general business.

GENERAL BUSINESS

In general business the chairperson must remember that adjourned or special business listed, and notices of motion, take precedence over all other business.

A **notice of motion** is a device used to make certain that all members are forewarned about a subject to be discussed at a specific meeting. The notice is given at one meeting but is not discussed until the subsequent meeting. In the meantime each member has received either the minutes listing this notice, or a separate written notice. This gives all members a chance to attend and put their point of view. Giving each member time to think about the subject ensures that a good debate is mounted and that the will of the majority will indeed be found.

At the subsequent meeting, a seconder is called for and if one is found the matter comes under discussion. If a seconder is not willing to make such a move, the motion lapses. This saves a great deal of useless argument, and good deal of time at the meeting itself.

A notice of motion is used only for matters of vital importance to the club: a change in the constitution perhaps, or a change in the amount of the subscription payable.

Further business

After dealing with the items of general business listed on the agenda the chairperson says 'Members, are there any further items you wish to discuss?'. This is the last-but-one stage of the meeting, but in a lively membership there will be many matters brought forward.

SOME USEFUL PROCEDURES

During all business, members stand, address the chair, give their motions in the affirmative, a seconder is called for and the motion is open for discussion along the lines of a mini-debate, with speakers to the motion being alternately **negative** and **affirmative** (see Appendix 2). At a meeting a negative point of view is presented first; in a debate it's the other way round. No chairperson should allow discussion before the motion is formed, as this is simply time-wasting. The motion's careful wording allows members to think about the exact idea presented to the meeting, thus avoiding pointless, and often endless, comment. Detailed information about formal motions is set out in Appendix 3. In frequently encountered situations, however, three procedures will help to streamline meetings: amendment, right of reply, and point of order.

Amendments

Amendments to motions seem to confuse most members of clubs and for this reason are not used as often as they might be. An amendment is a useful tool. The important thing to remember is that any amendment changes the wording of the motion only slightly; if the amendment seeks to change the motion radically, it is really another motion being foreshadowed and should not be accepted by the chair.

44 Chairing and Running Meetings

CAN YOU TELL THE DIFFERENCE?

Meetings can get into strife if the chairperson fails to recognise the difference between a motion and an amendment.

If the amendment is really a **foreshadowed motion** the chairperson should rule it out of order. Such a ruling must be accompanied by reasons for the decision. Then the original motion is discussed.

If that motion is defeated another motion (the foreshadowed one, which sought to change the original motion substantially) may be accepted by the chair. The mover is generally the member who tried to move the rejected amendment. This motion is then discussed and voted upon.

More mistakes are made in the area of amendments and foreshadowed motions than in any other. It is impossible to handle two motions at the same time, and chairpersons have gone grey trying to do so.

Example The motion is 'that we hold a fete on Saturday, December 4 at the Church Hall at 3 p.m.'. The amendment (which also needs a mover and a seconder) is 'at 2 p.m.'. This changes only the time, not the central theme, of the motion already put forward. The amendment is discussed and put to the vote. It is carried, meaning that the majority wants the fete to begin at 2 p.m. The chairperson now reads out the amended motion (strictly speaking this is called the **substantive motion**): 'that we hold a fete on Saturday, December 4 at the Church Hall at 2 p.m.'. If there is no further amendment, the motion is put and voted upon.

You can see from this example that '3 p.m.' is actually deleted from the motion and replaced by '2 p.m.': only a minor change from the original. Many times you will hear a chairperson say, 'The amendment becomes the motion'. This is quite wrong. The amendment is just those few words, altering the motion but slightly. When the amendment is passed it becomes a component of the original motion, but it *never* replaces the motion.

The person in the chair may accept as many amendments as the members wish to move, but, as with motions, *care must be taken to accept only one at a time.*

Right of reply

The mover of any motion is given the right of reply by the chairperson at the end of the debate. If the motion has been amended, the right of reply is given at the close of the discussion on the first amendment. This is the last opportunity to comment on the original motion; otherwise further amendments might pile up, giving rise to different viewpoints not included in the original wording.

Example At the correct time the chairperson simply says, 'Mr Caridi, as the mover of the motion, would you care to exercise your right of reply?'. The mover is not obliged to do so, but it is a splendid chance to refute all arguments brought up against the idea under discussion. As all floor members are permitted to speak only once to a motion, the right of reply is the only second chance offered and ought, in my view, to be grasped firmly. No *new* matter may be

46 Chairing and Running Meetings

introduced in this second speech; nor will any alert chairperson allow *irrelevant* matter to be brought forward during this right of reply.

> ### 'OUT OF ORDER'
>
> When it becomes clear to any membership that the chairperson will not allow members to waffle on during debate, nor speak several times to one motion, good floor members will marshall their thoughts and arguments quickly, present them crisply, and hope for a quick result. If you do not grasp the message and try to speak again, the chairperson will rule you out of order, giving the reason. This is a time-saving device, and is part of correct meeting procedure.

Point of order

There is another piece of correct procedure that is a very useful tool for all floor members; it is called 'point of order' and is used to control the meeting, the chairperson – or both!

If at any stage the chairperson misses a point that ought to have been picked up or queried, a floor member may stand and simply say 'Point of order'; and then explain what has been missed.

Example One member has dared to speak twice to the same motion and the chairperson has failed to notice this. It is then that the wide-awake floor member says, 'Madam Chairman, point of order. Tina Dasopoulou has already spoken to the motion'. The point is well taken by the chair, the offending member called to order, and the meeting proceeds as before.

The conduct of a meeting 47

Remember 'point of order', for it is one of the handiest pieces of meeting procedure you will ever find.

IN PROGRESS

While all this has been going on, the secretary has been taking notes and perhaps attending to the tape recorder. The motions and decisions of the meeting in progress form the basis of the minutes that the secretary will prepare for the next meeting.

FINALLY

When all the further business has been dealt with, the chairperson announces the date of the next meeting of the club, its time and its venue, and then declares the present meeting closed, using the following formula: 'Thank you for your attendance. We will meet next on Tuesday, March 16, at 7.30 p.m. in the Guide Hall. I now declare this meeting of February 16 closed'.

5 THE ANNUAL MEETING

For any association the thought of the Annual General Meeting may loom ahead like an impossible wall to be scaled. There is no need at all for apprehension about it. Certainly you'll have some extra people at your meeting, and some elections to conduct; but all you need is preparation, which is what you do before every ordinary general meeting. The annual meeting simply means that you need a little more planning, so that nothing will complicate matters.

AGENDA

With the planning done, your agenda for the annual meeting (see boxed example, page 56) will look much like the agenda for an ordinary general meeting. The chairperson declares the AGM open, and welcomes guests and members. Apologies are accepted.

The minutes read (or previously circulated) are those of *last year's annual meeting*. They are read by the secretary and confirmed on a motion with a seconder and a vote taken, before being signed by the chairperson. If there is business arising from those annual minutes it is then dealt with.

Correspondence *addressed to the annual meeting* is called for, read by the secretary, and received by general consent or by a motion. Remember that only letters dealing with aspects of the annual meeting, or good wishes for the meeting itself, are to be read. Ordinary correspondence is kept for the next general meeting.

Usually you will find there is little business arising from the last annual meeting's minutes or from the correspondence. After all, a year has gone by and matters very often resolve themselves.

When you are planning the AGM, remember the golden rule: don't confuse the business of ordinary general meetings with the business of annual meetings.

ANNUAL REPORT

After the correspondence has been received the president (whether chairperson or not) presents the annual report. This is prepared in advance, either from a perusal of the year's minutes or from personal notes kept throughout the year of office. Sometimes the secretary helps to prepare the annual report, but it is not strictly necessary. The president is the spokesperson for the group and therefore should present to the AGM what she or he perceives as the year's events and results.

Before the meeting, the chairperson should arrange for a member to move the adoption of the annual report and for another to second it. This is a time-saving device and it also ensures that the two short speeches of the mover and seconder are well prepared. Just a few words are needed about the excellence (or opposite!) of the report and about the work achieved during the year.

At the conclusion of these remarks the mover says, 'I have much pleasure in moving the adoption of the annual report for 19...' The seconder uses the same conclusion, substituting 'seconding' for 'moving'.

ANNUAL FINANCIAL STATEMENT

After the annual report the treasurer presents the annual financial statement, concluding with the words: 'Mr Chairman, I move that this annual financial report be received and adopted'. This is seconded by a member (who has been forewarned) and a few kind words are said about the work of the treasurer.

ELECTIONS

The election of office-bearers follows.

If only one person has been nominated for each executive office there is obviously no need for an election to be held. Even so, another person should take over the chair (as a 'guest' chairperson) to declare all positions vacant and to announce the new office-bearers. It is ludicrous for the chairperson to have to say something like 'I declare myself re-elected for the next twelve months'.

For the purpose of electing their executive some clubs call a special meeting before the annual meeting; this streamlines the annual meeting, as a declaration of the results is then all that the guest chairperson has to do. Your constitution should cover this area, so consult it for this information.

If an election takes place the vote should be by **secret ballot** rather than by a show of hands. No one wants to be seen to vote against a friend even in a situation where another nominee is clearly a better choice. A secret ballot means an objective result, which is what all associations ought to seek.

Paper and pencils should be provided for secret ballots.

Two members not nominated for office should act as **scrutineers**, count the votes, and bring the result to the waiting guest chairperson. After declaring the results, the new president (who may also be the chairperson), vice-president (or senior and junior vice-presidents if your constitution calls for this distinction), secretary, treasurer, and any committee members, are duly installed. The guest chairperson vacates the chair, and the new chairperson takes over. The first duty of the incoming chairperson is to make a **statement of policy** for the year ahead.

SPECIAL AGM BUSINESS

After the statement of policy, matters that need to be discussed at the AGM are brought forward. These are particular pieces of business, for example:

- an alteration to the constitution
- an increase (or decrease!) in the subscription
- a change in the frequency of meetings.

Matters of less importance are debated at ordinary general meetings.

GUEST SPEAKER

The guest speaker is next on the agenda.

This special guest is introduced, usually by the new chairperson who, as a nominee for the office now held, has done a little homework about the person and the subject. This means that it is a gracious introduction, preparing the ground for a receptive audience.

At the conclusion of the speech the guest is thanked, usually by a member who has been asked in advance to carry out this task. A few well-chosen words referring to some aspect of the speech or to the speaker, is all that is needed. It must always be given with sincerity, so that the speaker (who in small clubs is likely to receive no payment) feels that the visit has been worthwhile. If a gift is to be presented, it is the duty of the mover of the vote of thanks to make the presentation.

COMBINED MEETINGS

If your organisation is having an ordinary general meeting as well as the annual meeting – and this is common practice – the time to commence the ordinary meeting is after the guest speaker has been thanked. This gives the guest speaker an opportunity to depart before the ordinary meeting begins. The new chairperson moves on to the agenda for the ordinary meeting, and goes through procedure in the normal fashion.

SEPARATE MEETINGS

In my opinion it is better to keep annual meetings and ordinary general meetings separate, as a combined affair tends to become confusing for guests and members alike. It often means a very late evening or afternoon, unnecessarily. It also means throwing your new chairperson to the lions.

Normally, with a week, a fortnight or a month to prepare for the first ordinary general meeting the initial nervousness felt by most new chairpersons has largely disappeared. This means that the vital first

56 Chairing and Running Meetings

meeting with a new person in the chair is a pleasure and not a nightmare. It should also be remembered that the AGM is an important meeting. It deserves a time of its own – and a better-than-average guest speaker, if this is possible.

CONCLUSION

At the conclusion of the AGM agenda the chairperson wishes the new executive and all members well for the year ahead and announces the date, time and place of the next *ordinary* general meeting. The new chairperson says, 'I look forward to seeing you all at our next ordinary general meeting and I declare this year's Annual General Meeting closed'.

AGENDA

ANNUAL GENERAL MEETING

1. Chairperson declares meeting open.
2. Chairperson welcomes members and guests, and introduces special or official guests.
3. Apologies.
4. Minutes of the last AGM.
5. Correspondence addressed to AGM.
6. President's annual report.
7. Treasurer's annual financial statement.
8. Election of office-bearers.
9. President presents statement of policy.

The annual meeting

10 Special AGM business.
11 Introduction of Guest Speaker.
12 Guest address.
13 Vote of thanks to Guest Speaker.
14 Close of meeting.
15 Date, place and time of next ordinary general meeting.

6 SPEAKING IN PUBLIC

Taking office in an association usually means that you will be called upon to speak in public. Office-bearers are often asked to speak on behalf of their organisations. In this age when media interviewers whip out microphones at the drop of a story it is as well to know something about the challenging and exciting field of public speaking.

Added to this of course are duties that you take on as a member of your executive. Reading minutes, chairing meetings, preparing and presenting reports, debating controversial motions – they all have an element of public speaking in them, and a relaxed, confident speaker is more convincing that a tense, nervous one. Large clubs often meet in large halls, and that means you need to be able to use your voice so that all members (even those who *will* sit at the back) may hear you clearly.

FACING THE CROWD

You may be confident and articulate when you are addressing a small group or sharing views in private, but how do you react when faced with a crowd of listeners? Do you hesitate, stammer, blush, waffle, become tongue-tied, shift your feet or perspire with nerves? Most people do, but take heart – you can be helped to help yourself.

Taking up the challenge is the first thing to do, because that decision will give you some confidence in yourself and in your abilities. Tell yourself you can do it – others have before you. Practise as much as you can, and soon it will *appear* effortless. For some, it never is: if you are one of these people, no matter how often you address meetings there will always be that nervousness before you begin to speak. If this is the case, cheer up: the pumping of the extra adrenalin is what you need to give that fine edge to your speech. It will disappear once you have begun. The late Laurence Olivier admitted to feeling nervous before every performance, so you are in splendid company.

BREATH CONTROL

Learn to control your breathing by practising deep breathing daily. That means deep-down diaphragmatic breathing, which will expand your lungs. *Don't* take sharp, shoulder-raising gulps of air. This will only compound your problems of control. With lung expansion, you'll discover that the nervous trembling in your voice will disappear. You will be in control of yourself.

The other bonus of deep breathing is that with more air in your lungs you will be heard right to the back of the hall. That deep, quiet breathing will also settle any butterflies. Take three deep breaths before you launch into your speech – this will relax you.

TAPED EVIDENCE

Once your breathing is under control, you will want to hear yourself as others hear you. Invest in a tape recorder. Use it. When you play back your speech you will be able to identify your mistakes or annoying mannerisms. Then you can work to eliminate them.

If you do not have access to a good tape recorder there is a simple way to listen to yourself: cover one ear and speak aloud. You will hear your voice almost in the same way as it would sound on a tape recorder. Your listeners hear your voice projected ahead, whereas you hear it from behind, because your ears are behind your voice. That does make a difference to its sound. Of course, it is not possible to re-play yourself with this method, so you do not have the same advantage of self-correction that a tape recorder offers.

Listening to yourself by either method can be a chastening experience. It will probably make you long to improve your speaking voice. Listen particularly to the way you sound the endings of your words. Those final consonants are important: words can change their meanings without their final 't', 'd' or 'g'. Listen especially for this habit of 'losing' final consonants, and make certain that you correct it. After all, there's not much point in speaking if you are not being understood, is there?

MIRROR IMAGE

Don't just listen to yourself – watch yourself too. It's not the easiest thing to do, but persevere, as it will pay dividends. You can correct annoying movements and get rid of those ugly mannerisms simply by becoming conscious of them. People watching you speak will be aware of your mannerisms and may find them irritating. Don't give them the chance. Present your speech in front of a mirror, and practise a warm and all-encompassing smile: you don't want it to come across as a nervous twitch!

REHEARSE ALOUD

Above all, say it aloud. Don't worry about amused members of your household – they may be envying your dedication. However idiotic these methods may sound to you, you simply cannot learn this art in your head: it must be vocal. The late actor Richard Burton was reputed to have shouted aloud from the peaks of Welsh mountains when he was young – to improve his voice, his tonal qualities and to rid himself of his Welsh accent. So what was good enough for a professional is certainly good enough for you.

Practising at home is a sound idea, because if you can convince yourself that you are worth hearing, you are well on the road to convincing others.

CONFIDENCE TRICKS

Give yourself confidence by telling yourself (over and over again if necessary) that you can speak well. Others have done it without any more talent than you possess. So can you. Remember the people you've heard speaking in public or on radio or television whom you thought were deplorable: you know you can do better than that. Catalogue a few of the worst, work out how to better their performance, and put those lessons to work for yourself. This will give you real confidence to inform and charm an audience.

Observe a good speaker in the same way. List the good points and try to pinpoint what was the most effective technique used. When you understand what that was, use it yourself, though never copy the idea or the movement or the trick slavishly. You are in the business of presenting *yourself* as well as your speech, so it must be a genuine you.

By far the best trick in the confidence book is to *thoroughly prepare* your speech, your talk or your vote of thanks. It is almost impossible to sound confident or convincing if you are not sure of your topic. Know the content like the back of your hand. If you know what you intend to say, even if you do not know the precise words you will use finally, you are well ahead. That nervous tension will vanish.

HITTING THE TARGET

Know your audience. Choose language that they will understand. Tailor your words to match the people you are addressing, and don't make too many assumptions about their knowledge of the subject.

Be conscious of the size of your audience, too: recounting a story to a friend is very different from addressing a large group of people, though you should use the same friendly manner to make an effective communication.

GOOD NOTES

With all that preparation you will easily produce some notes about the theme. Have with you those notes in point form, to use as a prop if necessary. Prepare small pieces of card that will fit into the palm of your hand, and refer to the notes when you need them. A swift glance at a sentence, a quotation or a key word will be sufficient to trigger off what you want to say.

>
> ## SPEAKING TO A MOTION
>
> The point-form method also works well when you are speaking to a motion. Quickly note a few points and use them to guide you in your support of (or argument against) the motion. In this way you won't forget an important point that, with an alert chairperson, you won't be permitted to make later on in the debate.

With practice, always providing that you *do* know your subject well, you will be able to dispense with notes altogether. Don't try that too soon: if you do and you are not satisfied with your performance, you will lose that confidence you have worked so hard to achieve.

Don't read your speech. At most, if it makes you feel more secure, have your speech on the lectern as you speak from your cards. *Don't* write out your speech and learn it by heart – it's hard to achieve a natural tone with a memorised speech, and as sure as sunrise you will forget it at some point, and be left horrified at your failure. Rely on your preparation and your notes.

No matter how long or short the speech is, plan an arresting opening and a well-rounded conclusion. You must instantly grab the attention of your audience, and you must leave them with something to think about at its conclusion. Often the middle of the speech will take care of itself.

FIRST WORDS

Always preface that interesting beginning by addressing the people to whom you are speaking. The office of the person in charge of the meeting takes precedence over everyone else attending – even important personages. So your address will begin with 'Madam Chairman ...' If a lord mayor, a mayor, a bishop, an archbishop or a shire president is present it is correct to address them specifically before completing the preliminaries with '... distinguished guests, ladies and gentlemen'. It is advisable to group everyone else together like that to avoid the trap of mentioning everybody you think is important among your listeners but causing offence by forgetting one. That could make a lifelong enemy for you quite unnecessarily.

If it is a small gathering, 'Mr Chairman, ladies and gentlemen' is quite sufficient. Having said that, take a deep breath, look around the people in the room, and launch into what you have so carefully prepared to say.

NEXT WORDS

This is where you produce that startling opening sentence. It might be simply 'It gives me much pleasure to introduce our guest speaker for this month', followed by some information about the speaker. It could just as well be a shattering attack, in succinct phrases and rousing words, on the government of the day.

In other words, whatever the occasion that opening sentence is vital, for it sets the tone for the rest of the address. Then build on that beginning. The content is up to you, but do try to have some sort of structure in the body of your speech. It must flow evenly or you will confuse your listeners and lose their interest. Don't digress from the subject of your address. Move logically from point to point, helped by your discreet cards, until you arrive at that graceful, prepared conclusion.

SUMMING UP

Although I advised you earlier never to learn your speech by rote this does not apply to your final sentence or sentences. Know that part by heart. When you come to the end of your remarks, dredge up from your memory that well-thought-out conclusion, look squarely at your audience, and *say* it with firmness and conviction. Never spoil the impact of your conclusion with a lame 'Thank you'. It is unnecessary: the audience should thank you for the trouble you have taken – you don't need to thank them for listening. Just sit down and leave them to ponder your ringing conclusion.

You'll notice by listening to others and in preparing your own speeches that it is much harder to finish than to begin. Be conscious of that and be firm with yourself about your closing comments. Be strict with yourself and don't waffle on, padding out what you have already stated. It is always better to leave people wanting to hear more, than it is to send them to sleep or bore them into insensibility.

TIME IS THE ESSENCE

Time your address at home, and always keep within the limit, which you may impose upon yourself or which may be given to you by the committee of the club you have been invited to address. *Stay within that timing*. You've all been to meetings where the chairperson is desperately passing notes to the speaker, hoping to cut the time she or he is taking to get to the point. Don't let that happen to you. An invitation to speak for five minutes or twenty-five minutes means what it says. No matter how much research you have done and how many facts you have to impart, time *is* of the essence and you should abide by it.

It is also an excellent form of discipline, for when you pare down your material you are often left with the gold and not the dross.

HUMOUR – A SERIOUS MATTER

The hardest aspect of speaking in public is concerned with humour. Do you have it, or do you not? If possible use a little in a longer speech, because light-heartedness, correctly used, will endear you to your listeners. So try to cultivate this art despite its pitfalls. But please, do not drag humour in when it bears no relevance to the topic in the main body of the address. An ill-chosen and ill-timed joke is no joke at all. Aim for a news item, local event, or a personal experience that will underline in a happy and memorable fashion the point you are making. You'll be comfortable with this, and so will your audience. No one likes to be embarrassed by contrived humour.

WHEN YOU'RE SMILING

Smile at your audience. Don't be so overcome by nerves that your face stays tense. All those tiny muscles around your mouth are longing to relax into a welcoming smile. When this happens you'll have a much better rapport with your listeners, who will be drawn to you by your warmth.

THE EYES HAVE IT

After that, *look at your audience*. Really look at them, using your eyes. Don't stare fixedly at some spot on the back wall or at the ceiling.

Eye rapport is very important. Constant practice will mean that you are able to encompass your entire audience with your eyes, and appear to be speaking to each person individually. If – heaven forbid! – they are listening unwillingly, you will be able to fix them with your beady eye. When they listen willingly, you will want to share your thoughts most directly with them. This is possible only through eye contact.

Try to avoid looking at one person. Move your head, and thus your eyes, around the assembly. Don't swivel your whole body, or swivel like a robot; move naturally so that you are really looking at the people to whom you are speaking. Of course you are not speaking to each one personally, but the impression conveyed is that you are. Because they have this feeling of direct contact, the audience will appreciate what you are saying much more. They may afterwards even remember something of what you said – perhaps for ever. That is really the proof of this particular pudding.

YOUR VOICE

If your voice is not normally expressive, work on it. Pretty soon you will be able to use it as a musician uses an instrument. When you are conscious of the varying tones of your own voice you'll be able to convey various shades of feeling and meaning in the words you are using. This not only makes them mean much more to those who are listening to you, but it also makes it easier for you to convey your *exact* meaning. Be aware of all the elements you can use to produce a good voice.

Pitch

Try to pitch your voice at the right level so that it is neither too loud nor too soft; you want to be heard by everyone present, but you don't want to shout at them. If you do fall into that trap you will be remembered as someone who talked *at* them and not *to* them. Aggression from the platform rarely goes down well; indeed, it will often damage your cause. At the same time, to get your points across to your audience, pitch your voice a little higher than usual. This gives it a carrying note, so that what you say may be heard clearly.

Pace
Speak a little more slowly than you do normally. This gives your listeners time to catch up with what you are saying, and is a good safeguard against racing nervously through your speech.

Contrast
Try for contrasting light and shade in your voice, to avoid speaking in a boring monotone. This is a hazard for the nervous or inexperienced speaker, and nothing loses an audience more quickly.

Emphasis
Use a little more emphasis than you would in everyday conversation. In that way your voice, and the facts you are presenting, will be more clearly understood than if you mumble or gabble or don't emphasise key words.

Sincerity and vitality
Your voice should always convey friendliness and the pleasure you feel at being where you are, making this particular speech. If you can get across a sense of energy and vitality with your voice, so much the better. The strength of your convictions will be so much more compelling when you can manage this. It means that your sincerity will shine through everything you are saying.

Naturalness

Above all, be natural. Don't 'put on' a voice or a manner of speech or an accent that is not your own. Affectations don't impress – they have the opposite effect. Your voice and your manner should reflect your own personality, heightened *just a little* for good presentation.

The microphone

If a microphone is provided speak about 15 centimetres back from it and use your usual tone of voice as though your entire audience is seated in the front row.

STANDING ORDERS

Stand tall

Position yourself so that you are comfortable on your feet. Stand firmly but not rigidly. Have one foot a little in front of the other, because this gives you a better stance than placing your feet together. It also helps you to keep your body erect.

Put your shoulders back to expand your lungs. All that extra air you are then able to accommodate will improve the quality of your voice, and its control.

Are you swaying?

Be certain you are not swaying from side to side. It's possible to do this under stress and not to know that it is becoming a habit. When you are practising your speech, ask a relative or a friend to watch you particularly for this fault. In that way you can correct it before the habit gets out of control.

Where are your arms?

Ideally your arms should be held loosely at your sides, but nervousness often prevents this. Often arms and hands seem to have lives of their own. If you find that you are waving your arms about too much, put one behind your back to curb the tendency. You can clench and unclench that hand all you like; no one will notice it in that position. But please don't stand with your arms folded across your chest – nothing looks quite so casual, nor serves you so poorly.

Gestures

By all means use gestures, but make sure they are spontaneous and natural, not rehearsed and wooden. Be wary, however, of too many: if you illustrate every point and phrase with arm or body movements your listeners will be following your movements and not your words. This is the opposite of what you want to achieve.

The lectern

If there is a lectern, use it. Put your notes on it where you can see them easily. Look over the lectern if you are tall; but if you are short, stand to one side of it – your audience wants to see *you*, not just the top of your head. If you feel like a little support, grasp the lectern firmly, but never lean on it. If you lean on a table or lectern you will appear nonchalant and it will be more difficult to gain the confidence of your audience; they will equate your slovenly attitude with your speech.

YOU HAVE BEEN WARNED

Be forewarned about two very important 'don'ts'.

Never apologise
Even if you have been given precious little time to prepare yourself for the occasion, *don't* begin your address by saying so and apologising for your lack of preparation. If you do, most of your listeners will judge what you say from that defensive position and will find it wanting. Simply sail into your speech with every appearance of confidence and long preparation, and the odds will be in your favour.

Never announce your conclusion
Towards the end of your speech (and you are the only person to know that you are coming to the end), *don't* say 'In conclusion ...', 'My final point ...', 'In summing up ...', 'Just one more thing to say ...' or 'Finally ...'

You are in effect announcing that you've all but finished. You'll be almost wafted off the stage by the collective sigh of relief; you'll be deafened by the rustling of papers and the snapping of handbags; the shuffling of feet as people prepare to depart will shock you. Through all this commotion and mental relaxation, your audience will miss that wonderful conclusion you have worked so hard to perfect. You have just scuttled your speech.

Be warned: consult your notes, work your way through your points and then lead yourself without announcement to that carefully memorised final statement that will leave your listeners, not relieved that you have finished, but wishing to hear more of you.

NOW YOU'RE READY

Can you answer 'Yes' to all of these?

- Your preparation has been extensive. You have plotted your speech so that it has a startling introduction, a logical development of theme, and a rounded conclusion – without a last 'thank you' to mar its glory.
- Your appearance is groomed, comfortable and relaxed.
- You have worked on your voice.
- Your manner is confident.
- You can say what you want to say in words that convey their exact meaning and carry the most conviction.
- Your timing is precise.
- You are in control of yourself.

TAKE THE STEP

So what's next? Doing, of course.

Theory is all very well, but it is the practise that counts most in turning you into a splendid speaker, not just a competent one. The way to improve is to *do* it. Speak in public whenever you are asked, on whatever subject, so long as you feel you can research it sufficiently and deliver it with sincerity.

When you are asked to accept nomination to the executive of your organisation, *say yes*. Move motions and speak to motions whenever you can. Introduce guest speakers, thank speakers, and accept opportunities to speak on behalf of your club. Do anything that will let you exercise your newly found skills. It is hard work, but the rewards for your own self-esteem are considerable and completely worthwhile. Any chance you have to develop fluency and confidence is yours for the grasping. Even if practice does not make perfect, it certainly helps.

NOT TO THE MANNER BORN

Remember that public speakers are not born: they are made – by diligent practice, by trial and error, and by a willingness to participate.

Good public speakers take care to avoid clichés or the popular word or phrase of the moment. Don't let yourself copy-cat the worst of current usages.

Good speeches are made by speakers being willing to use words that mean exactly what they want them to mean, and to experiment with colourful speech.

AVOIDING THE CLICHÉ

The following letter was published in the Melbourne *Age* 23 August 1991. It underlines, by the clever use of clichés and worn-out usage, the need for speakers and writers to choose their phrases carefully.

> At this point of time, I take up my pen to support the valiant efforts of those who object to the rash of clichés that are now so widespread across the board, communications-wise. I can only hope that politicians and members of the media are addressing the problem, and that some sort of reform is in

> the pipeline and has not been put on hold. Let us hope, too, that we are about to encounter a J turn in standards of expression and erudition, and that we may once more find ourselves on a literary level playing field.
>
> Alternatively, caring and concerned educationists may seek to broaden the parameters of classroom interface and so effect some upsize in the literacy potential of their charges from now on in, or at worst, down the track.
>
> Hopefully, my comments will not elicit a negative knee-jerk response, and that I will be spared the necessity of writing back-to-back letters on the subject.
>
> J. Landy, East Malvern
>
> Are you guilty?

Successful public speakers *want* to be interesting. They are prepared to meet the challenge of delivering an argument, moving a motion, or presenting a speech in the best possible way to inform and engage others.

Skilful speakers gain and hold attention. They are people who speak with conviction, leaving no doubts in the minds of their listeners.

ARE YOU A PUBLIC SPEAKER?

Of course you are. If you prepare carefully and accept each challenge you will have become one before you are truly aware of it. You will want to accept each challenge and be ready for the next and the next – a little more confident each time, a little happier with each occasion, and a better speaker than you were before.

THE M AND P CHECKLIST FOR PUBLIC SPEAKERS

Be mindful of:

- **MATTER** – material, facts, sources of information, insight. Keep it simple, relevant and accurate.
- **MANNER** – logic, success in communicating, persuasiveness, sympathy with audience. Keep it friendly and sincere.
- **METHOD** – organisation of the speech itself, ingenuity in presentation and attack. Keep it grammatical and exact.

Be persuaded by:

- **PREPARATION** – essential, no matter how experienced you become
- **PRACTICE** – vital to every speaker
- **PACE** – keep your delivery slow enough for your audience to follow you
- **PAUSES** – use them well, to allow your audience to take in what you are saying, and for dramatic effect
- **PITCH** – is necessary for your voice to carry. Project your voice so that you are heard easily.
- **PUNCH** – your delivery needs it to deliver your conviction and carry your argument. Punch comes into its own when you utter your final sentence.

7 ANSWERS TO YOUR QUESTIONS

With the help of Chapters 1–6 you will feel confident to take your place within the framework of your particular club. But ... at those expertly conducted meetings problems will still arise.

Most of these sticky situations are covered here in the form of questions and answers in four broad categories. After you have digested this chapter you should feel able to deal with any crisis.

EXECUTIVE AND MEMBERS

Q. We are having trouble at Inner Wheel in finding people willing to take executive positions. Is there an answer to this problem?

A. It is never easy, as people do seem to be reluctant to take positions of responsibility. Many feel that they will be inadequate to the task, but usually the person elected to the executive rises to the challenge.

Try having, as well as a vice-president, an assistant secretary and an assistant treasurer. This means that you have executives in training. I was once in a club where the treasurer was confined to a wheelchair. He was brilliant at figures, but had some difficulty carrying out the tasks that required him to be mobile. We appointed an assistant treasurer who did all that part of the work. She eventually became the treasurer, having learned much while being a helper. This had been the thought farthest from her mind when she accepted the assistant's job.

Q. In our branch of the YMCA we have a vice-president and an assistant secretary. They don't seem to do much, and I was wondering just what they should do.

A. Both offices give opportunities for training for a future time when those office-bearers may fill the top positions on the executive. A vice-president and an assistant secretary (or assistant treasurer for that matter) are there to help with the duties expected of the executive members: whenever office-bearers are looking for assistance it is to their assistants that they turn.

It is also a learning opportunity; it's always a sensible idea for executive members to absent themselves occasionally so that the assistants have a chance to go it alone.

Q. Are the rules of meeting procedure set in concrete?

A. The formal motions are, but there is some leeway in the manner in which you conduct your meetings. This depends on the person in the chair. In my view it is better to follow the rules. If it is possible to be formal but informal at the same time, this would be ideal. As situations are seldom ideal, conduct your meetings in a friendly manner, but always knowing the rules of procedure and following them. If anything contentious arises you are then armed to deal with it quickly and expertly.

Q. Why do meetings have the reputation of being dreary? Our Trefoil Guild meetings are fun.

A. I'm delighted to hear it. Meetings should always be enjoyable to attend, not dull and dreary. I am sure that your membership knows its meeting procedures, exercises them, extends the chairperson's role by keeping up with what is happening, debates clearly every issue before it, and looks for the entertaining side of being together with a common aim.

If all chairpersons would relax, enjoy themselves, admit mistakes when they are made, seek help if flummoxed, and delegate some authority, organisations would benefit enormously. Dreariness would vanish. The time saved by avoiding futile arguments and discussions would amaze and delight members.

When meetings are informative, interesting, productive, structured and efficient, they are good to attend. That way lies achievement, success for your organisation, and fun.

Q. In your opinion just who is responsible for making sure that a meeting helps achieve the aims of a club? The person in the chair?

A. No. Every member of every club is responsible for the quality of the meeting. Every member should know what is going on in that organisation and every member should contribute. It is useless complaining about your chairperson if you do not support that office in every way you can. Follow the agenda, follow the structure of the meeting, and help your chairperson if she or he is struggling with some convoluted piece of business. Good floor members make good groups, and that makes for satisfaction all round, and for achievement of the organisation's aims.

Q. When we have elections in our Rostrum Club we do not have a seconder for each nomination. Is it always necessary to have nominations seconded?

A. Your constitution should cover the method of carrying out annual elections. In my view, it is sensible to have a seconder for a nomination, because it ensures that each nominee has the support of at least two people. If members make nominations without a seconder, many names can be brought forward, few of them with any support. The ballot takes much longer if this is the case.

If the constitution of your organisation does not have clear guidelines for the annual elections, you should amend the document to include such instructions.

Q. At our Rotary Club the secretary reads the annual report at the AGM. Is this correct?

A. No. The president is the spokesperson for your club and has the right to read and present the annual report. The secretary may be consulted when the report is being prepared, so that nothing is omitted, but this does not entitle that office-bearer to present it.

Q. The minutes the secretary of our Choral Society writes are so long that we are running out of storage space. What can we do?

A. Point out the problem, tactfully. Have a good look at the style of the minutes. Probably they record every tiny detail. This is not necessary; for instance when a motion is lost, the secretary need record only that fact: 'Sue Tan moved, Joe da Silva seconded, that the choir has supper after each rehearsal. The motion was lost'. No action has to be taken, so the bald fact is sufficient.

If your secretary records every argument for and against, she or he is possibly over-writing in all areas, and this is why the minutes are so verbose.

Q. The secretary of our Kindergarten Auxiliary does not bring copies of her outgoing correspondence to our meetings. Should she do this? I am interested to see them.

A. So you should be. She may be writing ill-spelt, ungrammatical letters or not writing at all, for all you know. This is not a good image for your auxiliary to have in your community. At your next meeting, just move a motion 'that all outgoing correspondence be presented at each meeting', and see if your fellow members support you. If they do, your secretary will be required to table the outgoing as well as the incoming correspondence.

If you find that she is not representing you as you would wish, vote her out of office at your next election.

Q. Our Lions Club treasurer often claims to have used petty cash for parking meters. Then he forgets to replace it. What can we do?

A. Have a tactful word with him, to stop this habit. If it persists, vote him out of office at the next AGM.

Q. I am president of our branch of the Jaycees, and we have a very shy member. How can I help him to enjoy our meetings more, and bring him out of himself?

A. Do you have name tags at your meetings? If you do, put him in charge of those. As he gives them out, he naturally learns the names of all members and has to respond to their pleasantries. When a discussion is taking place, consciously ask him for his opinion. If you have a tea and coffee roster make sure every member has a turn, but perhaps put him in charge of keeping supplies up to date.

Because you are aware of the problem you will probably find other small ways to make him feel wanted and comfortable in your group.

Q. At our Red Cross meetings I never seem to be given a chance to speak. What should I do?

A. Raise your hand before you wish to speak so that you will be noticed from the chair. If this still doesn't gain you attention, mention the matter privately to your chairperson.

Q. The president of our CWA branch always represents the branch when conferences are held at State level. Wouldn't it be a good idea to appoint **delegates**?

A. Check your constitution. It could very well stipulate that the president must perform this duty, as she is the spokesperson for your particular branch. If there is no such restriction in place, perhaps it would be a good idea to move that some extra delegates attend the next conference. In that way you might get a better spread of information from the event. You might also educate some members in the ways of the CWA at this State level. Such affairs often engender enthusiasm in those participating, and that is always beneficial to your branch.

MOTIONS

Q. Our chairperson always says that the minutes may be confirmed by a motion from 'two members who were present at the last meeting'. Is this right?

A. No. When the chairperson calls for a motion to confirm the minutes, there is a pause during which any member may query the content of the minutes. If there is no criticism, or alteration needed, it means that the minutes are a true record of all that happened at the previous meeting. That being so, any member, whether present or not on that occasion, may move or second the **confirmation of the minutes**.

Q. Why does a lost motion have to be recorded? If it doesn't give our Mothers Club secretary any following-up to do, it need not be in the minutes at all, surely?

A. It seems to me that a succinct note of any **unsuccessful motion** should be made. This proves what took place at the meeting, and it serves as a record for the future. For example, if nothing is recorded and Val Compassi, a new member, reads the minutes and sees no mention of closing the tuckshop at recess, which she thinks is a good idea, she could well move that same motion again, unwittingly. This is time-wasting, as the membership has already voted against this motion.

Q. Often at our Guide meetings a motion is moved and seconded, and then withdrawn. I don't think we are handling this well. What is the right method?

A. To withdraw a motion the consent of the mover, the seconder, and the unanimous consent of the membership, are all needed. Once a subject has been raised it is up to those present to say whether it should be withdrawn or not, as that particular thought might have triggered off something important in the minds of some members. They are entitled to have it discussed. It may well be lost, but that does not alter the right of members to a debate on the topic.

Q. What happens to a withdrawn motion then? Does it have to be shown in the minutes?

A. In **recording a withdrawn motion** it is correct to write (for example): 'Bill Wagner moved and Josie O'Mara seconded that a letter of criticism be written to the City Council. On the unanimous vote of members, the motion, after discussion, was withdrawn'. Detail is not needed. If all the details of the discussion were recorded it would defeat the purpose of its withdrawal, which is to demonstrate that the membership voted the matter to be of little significance. It would be like going casually into a room and going out again, but leaving some possessions behind to prove you were there.

Q. One of the knowledgeable members of our CWA keeps talking about original and substantive motions. What on earth are they?

A. The **original** motion is the one first put before the meeting. If the motion is amended it is then called the **substantive** motion. If there are lots of amendments before the final vote, the motion is called the **resolution**. It's not essential to use these three terms; you are acting competently if you simply handle the motion correctly.

Answers to your questions

Q. The other day at the YMCA gym meeting I moved 'that we do not have a barbecue this year' and was ruled out of order. I was too stunned to ask why.

A. Your motion was **in the negative**, so it was pointless. If nothing is moved, nothing is done. An affirmative motion, 'that we organise a barbecue for September 4 at 12.30 p.m.' is a positive statement, and can be acted upon.

Q. I thought that all motions had to be in an affirmative form. When a past president of our Soccer Club moved 'that the question be not now put' I thought he was out of order, but the chairperson accepted it.

A. This is the one exception to that affirmative rule. Sometimes called '**the previous question**' (see Appendix 3), the objective of this motion is to prevent a vote being taken on a motion before the chair; in other words, it would **shelve the motion**. It is not often used, but it is handy to know about it. The motion must be seconded, and is moved only when a motion is under discussion (not when an amendment is being aired). There is no right of reply, and the mover should be a person who has not previously spoken on the matter.

If the meeting decides to shelve the motion, that is, to uphold 'the previous question', it cannot be brought forward again at the same meeting.

Q. What about at a later meeting? Can a motion that has been shelved be discussed then?

A. Yes, it may be introduced at a subsequent meeting.

90   Chairing and Running Meetings

Q. What happens if the meeting decides it doesn't want to abandon the motion, and wants to vote on the matter?

A. Without any further discussion, after the motion known as 'the previous question' has been lost, the chairperson must put the original motion to the vote.

Q. Does the chairperson have to accept this motion of 'the previous question'?

A. No, there are discretionary powers allowed in this instance. But, as always, the will of the majority of members must prevail. The chairperson is in the hands of the members.

Q. When is the best time to speak to a motion you have moved? I've noticed that one of our YMCA members always waits until his motions are seconded before he puts his case.

A. Either way is correct. In my view it is better to speak to your motion immediately. If you make your points at once, in doing so you are likely to encourage a seconder, thus opening it up for debate. If you state your motion baldly and do not elaborate or support your idea in any way your motion may lapse for want of a seconder. What a waste!

Q. What about the person who seconds a motion?

A. The same thing applies. The seconder may speak to the motion immediately or reserve the right to speak later on. In my view the seconder ought to grasp the opportunity to speak immediately, making the points as clearly and as succinctly as possible, to help the mover of the motion persuade the membership to accept that course of action.

Q. What does 'pro forma' mean, and when is it used?

A. If a mover has trouble finding a seconder, a person who is not too sure of the intention of the motion may second it **pro forma**. This is really saying 'I'm not sure what this is all about, but I am interested enough to second it so that discussion may take place'. It saves a motion from lapsing for want of a seconder, and opens up the matter for debate.

Q. Our Scouts Association always seems to take longer to discuss motions than any other club I belong to. I can't work out why. Could you help me solve this?

A. I am willing to bet that your Association's chairperson is allowing everyone to speak to the motion. That's very time-consuming. Speakers should be **alternately negative and affirmative**, so that the discussion works like a mini-debate (see Appendix 2). If every speaker is in support of the motion and thinks it's a fine proposal, there's no point in going on and on: it's too repetitive, and wasteful of time and energy. Put the motion, have it passed, and go on to the next business on the agenda.

If you find yourself in this situation, keep your chairperson to the debate formula.

Q. How do I do that?

A. When you find that the speakers are not introducing new matter during their support or criticism of the motion and your chairperson

92 Chairing and Running Meetings

seems unaware of this, move 'that the question be now put'. This will close the debate, allow the vote to be taken, and the meeting to proceed.

Q. Just last week at the Church Guild meeting I did not agree with the chairperson's ruling but I did not know how to handle it. Can you help?

A. A ruling from the chair is usually taken as final, but it may be challenged. You do this either by a motion of dissent, or a vote of no confidence.

Q. What's a motion of dissent?

A. A **motion of dissent** is a motion against a particular ruling, and not against the chairperson's usual handling of the meeting. It is treated like any other motion – that is, it needs a mover and a seconder.

A new chairperson, usually the immediate past occupant of the chair, is named to handle this motion only. The usual chairperson, now in the body of the meeting, states the reasons for the ruling. The mover of the motion of dissent explains the reasons for disagreement with this ruling.

If the motion of dissent is upheld, the chairperson resumes the chair and reverses the previous decision and ruling. If the motion of dissent is lost, the chairperson resumes the chair and simply carries on with the business in hand, without any further censure from members.

Q. And the vote of no confidence – how does that work?

A. This **vote of no confidence** or **no-confidence motion** is used very rarely indeed, as most clubs would prefer to muddle through until the next AGM rather than create a fuss. But when it *is* used it is because the chairperson has proved to be hopelessly incapable, biased or utterly inefficient. If the vote is carried then the chairperson *must* resign. It is seldom used, because it is seldom needed. Most chairpersons try their level best to be impartial; most are efficient (or nearly so); and most are trustworthy – thank goodness!

AMENDMENTS

Q. At our Senior Citizens group we still argue about amendments. Would you clarify them?

A. Remember that an amendment changes the idea of the motion only slightly, by altering a few words, or deleting or adding a few words. Beware the lengthy amendment: it usually has a trap for the unwary somewhere. This trap is that it seeks to change the motion too much to be acceptable as an amendment. Watch out for the **negative amendment** – one that is a direct negative to the motion – and don't accept it. A vote registered against the original motion has the same effect.

Remember too that each amendment needs a different mover and a different seconder.

There is no limit to the number of amendments. Just be careful not to have too many clauses attached to the motion. Sometimes this complexity makes it very difficult for members to vote in the way they would wish.

The other trick about amendments is to stop worrying about them, and to use them to good effect.

Q. We have someone in our Parents and Friends Association who is always moving amendments to motions. How many amendments can each member move to each motion?

A. No member may move or second more than one amendment to each motion. If your member persists in whittling away at motions, use your wonderful 'point of order' tool to point out this hard-and-fast rule. If you feel a little diffident about doing this at the meeting, tell your chairperson privately about the rule.

Q. Are you allowed to speak to an amendment when you have already spoken to the motion? Our Legacy chairperson will not allow this.

A. Your chairperson is incorrect. You may speak again. Each amendment is treated as a separate entity, so all present may speak to each amendment.

Q. At our last Soroptimists meeting we had before the chair a motion 'that we hold a garden party on November 7 at Government House and that we invite the Hawthorn Soroptimists to join us'. We had a lot of trouble with this and could not seem to achieve a result pleasing to everyone. Was there something wrong with the motion?

A. Yes and no. With two **clauses** like that in the original motion it can be tricky. If some of your members did not want to include Hawthorn in your plans they would want to vote *for* the first clause but *against* the second.

It could have been handled well if an alert floor member had spotted the problem and moved an amendment to delete 'and that we invite the Hawthorn Soroptimists to join us'. As this was obviously not done the chairperson had the option of accepting the first clause as the original motion. Once that was passed, the second clause (**foreshadowed** in the original motion) could have been moved. Then the will of the majority would show up clearly, especially if that second motion were lost.

Q. At our Nursing Association meeting we all voted to drive our own cars on our calls. After that had been enshrined in the minutes we seemed to change our minds about it. How do we go about taking that motion off our books?

A. You need to **rescind the motion** about your cars. This you do by sending a **notice of motion** to each member, outlining exactly what the motion was and the date on which it was passed. This notice will give everyone time to think through the various aspects of driving your own cars.

A notice of motion takes precedence on the agenda, following only adjourned business.

If the motion to rescind is won, the previous motion is declared null and void. If the motion to rescind is lost, the original motion on the books is still valid – and you will drive your own cars.

Q. Could we have rescinded the motion at the same meeting? We seemed to cool off very quickly.

A. No. If you moved a motion and then rescinded it at the same meeting, the result would be chaos. Even one meeting later the same chaos could result. After some weeks have gone by, and if the association still feels an error of judgement has been made, the notice of motion is sent. If a **rescission** is brought forward in this correct manner, everyone has had time to think.

Q. The chairperson of our Apex Club ruled that a motion can be rescinded only when the mover and seconder of that motion in question are present. I didn't think this was right, but I didn't know why. Can you tell me?

A. Of course you were right. Had the chairperson been correct it would have meant that motions have to stay on the books for ever if the mover or the seconder has left the club for whatever reason. It is the will of the membership that is important here. A motion to rescind is treated in exactly the same way as any other motion. The vote decides whether a change is made or not.

Q. I was chairing an Apex meeting recently and someone moved 'that the question be now put'. I was lost, as I had not heard the motion used before and did not know how to handle it. Help!

A. Most times discussion does not become tedious and this formal motion is not needed. You must have allowed the debate to drag on at that meeting. The motion, which simply indicates that the debate is being gagged, often happens at the right time, when arguments are becoming repetitive. Members may even interrupt a speaker if the boredom is too great – and get away with it. A seconder is not needed. There is no discussion allowed on 'that the question be now put': this is a safeguard against further boring and repetitive talk! This motion may be used either on an amendment or a motion and is voted upon forthwith. If the formal motion is carried, the motion interrupted by this formality is then put to the floor immediately, subject only to the right of reply being exercised.

Q. What happens if 'that the question be now put' is not upheld by the membership?

A. The discussion of the original motion is resumed. You will find, however, that the formal motion is usually carried, for it is moved from the floor only when things become exceedingly dull or appear to be achieving very little – or nothing.

RULES

Q. Our Junior Cricket Club doesn't have a constitution. We seem to muddle along happily without one. Should we do something about it?

A. Yes, I think you should. While you are getting along without a statement at the moment, if you were to get into trouble you would really need that constitution to help you to resolve it. No good chef would set about creating a dish without a recipe. In the same way, each group needs its own set of rules to make its organisation work well. The guidelines set down in a constitution are there to help your club, not to restrict it. Look upon your constitution as your master recipe, refer to it when in doubt – and relax, secure in the knowledge that your constitution is there to assist you and support you if troubles arise.

Q. The chairperson closed the meeting of our Tennis Club and at once allowed members to speak about a tournament. What should I have done?

A. You should have said 'Point of order', explaining that the meeting was closed. This would have brought your chairperson and those out-of-order players into line. A clear distinction should always be made between meeting business and what might be raised informally. Discuss it over a cup of tea instead.

98 Chairing and Running Meetings

Q. When a point of order is made, how quickly does the chairperson have to rule on it? The chairperson at our Zonta group seems to dither for ages.

A. That's not unusual. The truth is that the ruling on a **point of order** should be made immediately. Whether upholding the point or rejecting it, the chairperson should give the reasons for doing so. The members then know and understand what is happening. It's also a painless way of learning meeting procedures!

Q. The other night at the Young Farmers the mover and seconder were each given a right of reply. Is this right?

A. No, it's incorrect. The **right of reply** is given by the chairperson to the mover of the original motion – not to the seconder and not to the mover of any subsequent amendment.

Q. Why is it necessary to have a right of reply at all?

A. Well, it's a means of answering any objections raised during the discussion. No new matter is allowed to be introduced – just rebuttal of points brought forward against the motion. It also finishes the debate, as no more comment is permitted after the right of reply. Immediately the speaker has concluded her or his remarks the chairperson calls for the vote to be taken.

Q. If someone tries to speak after a right of reply has been given, what should be done? It happened to me as chairperson of our Heritage committee and I was unsure about what to do.

A. You should have ruled the speaker out of order, explaining that the right of reply is the very last word heard before the vote is taken. Do it with tact, but *do* it. If you don't, the discussion will drag on, the same arguments will be brought forward again, and the debate will not reach its conclusion.

Q. At last month's Council meeting the mayor, who was in the chair, was given the casting vote. She then supported the new idea contained in the motion. Should she have done this?

A. Most definitely not. When called upon to exercise **the right of a casting vote**, the mayor, as chairperson, *must* **vote with the status quo**. That is, the casting vote cannot be used to introduce something different. By upholding what is in place already, the chairperson is seen to be with tradition. If the chairperson were to vote the other way, it would be on that vote alone that the motion was passed and that something new was set in train. This is not the chairperson's function: she or he must be impartial and so must not sway the meeting. Upholding the status quo and supporting 'what exists now' demonstrates that impartiality.

That the chairperson is also the mayor makes no difference to this ruling.

Q. At our Sporting Association meetings the chairperson sometimes seems to have two votes. He appears to know what he is doing, so I have not questioned this. Could he be right?

A. Yes, but only in an association that incorporates many different clubs. Let us suppose that all the basketball clubs in one area have a combined association and that the president of that conglomerate (your chairperson) is a member of the Mt Beauty club. As a Mt Beauty *delegate* he has a vote in general discussions; otherwise his area would not be represented and that would be unfair. But if a casting vote is needed according to the constitution of the Association of Basketball Clubs, as the *chairperson* he has to cast that final vote. In this instance he would be seen to be having two votes, but in fact he's wearing two hats. His club has the right to one vote, and the only time he as chairperson of the Association is called upon to vote is to give the casting vote that resolves the deadlock.

Of course the basketball chairperson knows that he must cast his vote against the motion, to retain the status quo.

APPENDIX 1
GUIDELINES FOR A SIMPLE CONSTITUTION

Adapt this format to suit the needs of your organisation.

NAME

The name of this Group (*or* Club *or* Committee) shall be...

AIMS

The aims of this group shall be:

1. to afford the opportunity for...
2. to raise money to be used for...
3. to encourage the use of...
4. to maintain the state of...
5. to practise the art of...
6. to help the...
7. to stimulate interest in...
8. to foster the playing of...

MEMBERSHIP

Membership shall be open to any person interested in the stated aims of this Group.

FINANCE

Each member shall pay an annual subscription of ... plus ... per meeting.

or

Each member shall pay an annual subscription of ... only.

MEETINGS

This Group shall meet twice monthly, on the second and fourth Thursday of each calendar month (with the exception of the month of January or any public holiday that falls on a normal meeting day), unless otherwise arranged by general consent of the membership. Ten members are necessary to form a quorum.

OFFICE-BEARERS

Office-bearers (the Executive) shall be:

President
Vice-president
Secretary
Treasurer
Programme Planner

In the absence of the President and Vice-president, the immediate past president shall accept responsibility for running the meeting.

Office-bearers shall be elected for a period of ... (months *or* years), and are eligible (*or* not eligible) for re-election for the consecutive term.

The President shall have (*or* not have) a casting vote.

NOMINATION AND ELECTION

Nominations for office-bearers shall be submitted in writing, with the consent of the nominee, prior to the Annual General Meeting.

or

Nominations, with the consent of the nominee, with a mover and seconder, shall be submitted in writing before the Annual General Meeting.

or

Nominations for office-bearers shall be submitted in writing, with the consent of the nominee, one month before the Annual General Meeting.

Elections shall take place at the Annual General Meeting.

or

Elections shall take place one month before the Annual General Meeting, with the new executive to be installed at the Annual General Meeting.

Voting shall be by secret ballot.

ALTERATION OR AMENDMENT TO THE CONSTITUTION

Alterations to the Constitution may be made only after Notice of Motion of the alteration has been sent to every member, one full month before the Annual General Meeting.

APPENDIX 2
THE RULES OF DEBATE

A debate is a contest between two teams, each consisting of three speakers, who try to persuade the listeners to accept the proposition they are advancing. The debate is controlled by a chairperson, who usually acts as the timekeeper also.

The team that takes the **positive** side, that is, argues *for* the proposal, is known as the **Affirmative**; the team that argues *against* the proposal is known as the **Negative**.

The affirmative team, which sits on the right side of the chairperson, begins the debate. The negative team, which sits to the left of the chairperson, ends the debate.

The three speakers work as a team, supporting each other's arguments and rebutting the opposition as often, and as forcefully, as possible.

The first speaker for the Affirmative should define the words used in the topic, outline the arguments the team will present, and begin to develop those points.

The first speaker for the Negative agrees or disagrees with the definition of the topic, rebuts any arguments already put forward, outlines the team plan, and begins to introduce arguments in favour of their negative case.

The second speakers for both the Affirmative and Negative should present the bulk of the new matter for their side of the debate, criticise the opposition's stance, and take every opportunity to reinforce their own argument by reasoned rebuttal.

The third speaker for the Affirmative demolishes all arguments brought forward by the opposition, refers back to the original case plan, adds to the points already made, contrasts the two sides of the debate, and sums up the affirmative's propositions.

The third speaker for the Negative restates the team's aims in the arguments, rebuts everything brought forward by the opposing side, and sums up the points brought forward in support of the negative side of the debate. This speaker *may not introduce any new matter*, and is penalised if this rule is broken.

HINTS

Some of the rules of debate need not be hard and fast, as initiative in presentation is encouraged; but they certainly serve as a useful beginning for any debating team. The following points are important.

- **Preparation** means time together to discuss the subject, and to prepare material so that arguments may be brought forward with conviction.
- A team *must* work together to achieve success.
- A good debater can construct an argument whether the topic appeals, or whether the side allocated suits her or his own viewpoint, or not.
- Carefully consider the **matter**, the **manner** and the **method** of your presentation.
- The order of the speakers is vital – the third speakers must have quick, argumentative minds so that they can speak at short notice, for they will have only the time given to the debate to marshal rebuttals and comment. Choose teams carefully and then decide, just as carefully, the order in which members speak.

APPENDIX 3
RULES AND EFFECTS RELATING TO FORMAL MOTIONS

The following four pages set out, in an easy-to-follow table, the rules and effects relating to formal motions (sometimes called **procedural motions** because they relate to the procedures that move the meeting on).

Two rules not listed in the table may help office-bearers and members using formal motions at their meetings.

- The chairperson has the discretion to reject both **the previous question** and **the closure**.
- The two **adjournment** motions may be amended, but only as to the time, the place or the date mentioned in the adjournments.

RULES FOR FORMAL MOTIONS

Type of motion	Can the speaker be interrupted?	Is a seconder required?
The previous question – 'that the question be *not* now put'	No	Yes
The closure – 'that the question be now put'	Yes	No – chairperson has discretion to accept without seconder
'Proceed to next business'	No	Yes
Adjournment of debate	No	Yes

continued on page 110

Appendix 3

Is any discussion allowed?	Can it be moved on both motion and amendment?	General remarks
Yes – and on the main motion too. Previous speakers may speak again.	No – on the main motion only.	If carried, the main motion may not be brought forward again at the same meeting. If not carried, a vote on the main motion is taken immediately.
No	Yes	If carried, right of reply is exercised by mover of original motion and vote is taken. If lost, discussion is resumed.
No	Yes	If carried, matter is disposed of for this meeting. If defeated, matter may be raised again at a later meeting.
Yes Previous speakers may speak again	Yes	If defeated, motion can be moved again after an interval. If carried, mover has the right to reopen debate when it is resumed.

continued on page 111

Type of motion	Can the speaker be interrupted?	Is a seconder required?
Adjournment of meeting	No	Yes
'That the question lie on the table'	No	Yes

Is any discussion allowed?	Can it be moved on both motion and amendment?	General remarks
Yes. Previous speakers may speak again.	Yes	If defeated, motion can be moved again after an interval.
Yes. Previous speakers may speak again.	Yes	There can be a later motion at the same meeting to take the question from the table.

GLOSSARY

agenda Programme used as the plan for a meeting.

amendment Minor change in the wording of a motion.

audit An examination of an organisation's financial matters, carried out by an independent body.

balance sheet See *financial statement*.

carried Term used when the affirmative vote outweighs the negative vote.

casting vote Vote given to the chairperson when the votes for a motion equal the votes against the motion.

constitution Set of written rules, designed to govern an organisation.

deadlock The situation that arises when equal numbers of votes are cast for and against a motion being discussed.

dissent A difference of opinion; a vote to withhold assent to a motion.

dues Fees paid on joining a club or organisation.

executive The group of people (president and/or chairperson, secretary, treasurer and delegated others) that leads an organisation.

financial statement Report of financial matters, prepared by the treasurer. Also called financial report or balance sheet.

general consent Term used when calling for a vote on a motion that is certainly acceptable; for example, 'Is it your wish that we receive the correspondence by general consent?'.

lie on the table Term used for the suspension of discussion of any matter before the membership.

lost Term used when the negative vote outweighs the affirmative vote.

minutes A written record of the business of a meeting.

motion Term used for any course of action to be considered by members of an organisation.

mover The person who moves a motion.

notice of motion Notice given at one meeting of a motion to be discussed at the next.

office-bearers The executive: the president (and/or the chairperson), secretary, treasurer and, in some cases, delegates.

petty cash A small amount of money kept by the treasurer (usually in cash) to cover everyday expenses.

point of order Term used to point out (to the chairperson) any incorrect procedure at a meeting.

president The head of an organisation, who usually, but not always, acts as chairperson at meetings.

previous question, the The name given to the motion 'that the question be not now put'. The only negative motion acceptable to the chairperson.

pro forma (Latin, 'as a matter of form') A term used by the seconder of a motion when she or he reserves full support of the motion but

114 Chairing and Running Meetings

believes that the discussion opened up by the seconding should take place.

quorum (Latin, 'of whom') The number or proportion of members needed at a meeting (as stated in the constitution) before business can be transacted.

rebuttal The use of convincing evidence to oppose an argument.

rescission The rescinding of a motion; that is, the removing of a motion from the minute book. This can be done after a notice of motion referring to the matter has been circulated among members.

resolution Term for a much-amended motion that has been accepted by a club or organisation.

right of reply The right given to the mover of a motion to speak again before the vote is taken.

scrutineer A person authorised to inspect the counting of votes at an election.

seconder The person who supports the mover of a motion, ensuring that the motion will be discussed.

secret ballot A system of voting in which votes are made in writing, not by a show of hands, to preserve secrecy.

special meeting A meeting called to discuss an extraordinary matter before the membership.

status quo (Latin, 'the state in which') A term used in meeting procedure to describe a situation as it is at present. Always used in the context of a proposed change.

withdrawal of motion The process by which a motion is cancelled after the mover, the seconder and the entire membership vote to do so.

INDEX

All glossary terms are in **bold**.

adjournment
  of debate 108
  of meeting 110
agenda 7–8, 51, 56–7, **112**
amendment 20, 43–5, 93–7, **112**
  constitutional 104
  foreshadowed 94–5
  negative 93
annual general meeting 49–57
  annual financial statement 53
  annual report 52, 84
  combined meeting 55
  conclusion 56
  elections 53–4, 103
  guest speaker 54–5
audit 30, **112**

balance sheet *see* financial statement

casting vote 12, 99, **112**
chairperson 96, 97, 98, 99
  definition x–xi
  duties 3–13, 39, 83
  no confidence 93
  qualities 14
  statement of policy 54
  voting 12, 99

closure 96, 108
constitution 4, 5, 9, 37, 38–9, 53, 54, 84, 86, 97, 101–4, **112**
correspondence 8, 19, 40–1, 51–2, 85

deadlock **112**
debating *see* public-speaking
dissent 11, 12, 92, **112**
dues **112**

elections 53–4, 84, 85, 103

financial statement 30, 31, 32, 41, 53, **112**
foreshadowed amendment 94–5
foreshadowed motion 44

general consent **113**
guest speaker 25, 54–5

lie on the table 110, **113**

meetings
  combined meeting 55
  conducting 37–47
  preparation 7
  procedures 82
  proceedings 9–13, 18–25, 32
  separate meeting 55–6
  special meeting 18
  see also annual general meeting

minute books 6
minutes 8, **113**
  confirmation of 39, 87
  follow-up 24–5
  reading 18–19, 38–9, 51, 84
  taking 19–20
  writing up 20–4
modes of address 38
motion 9–11, 32, 87–93, **113**
  dissent 11, 12, 92
  foreshadowed 44, 95
  formal (procedural) 107, 108–11
  lost (unsuccessful) 87
  mover 11, 52, 96, **113**
  no-confidence 92–3
  notice of 42, 95, **113**
  rescind 95
  seconder 11, 42, 52, 84, 88, 90, 96
  shelving 89
  speaking to 66, 90
  substantive 44–5, 88
  withdrawn 87, 88, **114**

notice of motion 42, **113**

office-bearers 6, **113**
out of order 46

petty cash 30, 85, **113**
point of order 46, 94, 97, 98, **113**
president 3, **113**
  see also chairperson
previous question 89, 90, **113**
pro forma 91, **113**

procedural motions 107
public-speaking 61–78
  breath control 62
  checklist 78
  notes 65
  order of address 66–7
  posture 72–3
  preparation and rehearsal 63–5
  rules of debate 105–6
  speaking to a motion 66, 90
  voice 70–2

quorum 9, 37, 102, **114**

rescission 95, **114**
resolution 20, 88, **114**
right of reply 11, 45, 98, **114**
right to speak 90

scrutineer 53, **114**
seconder 11, 42, 52, 84, 88, 90, 96, **114**
secret ballot 53, **114**
secretary 15–26
  duties 17–26, 38, 84, 85
  qualities 26
statement of policy 54
status quo 12, 99, **114**

treasurer 27–33
  duties 29–33
  qualities 33

voting 11–12, 99–100

withdrawal of motion 87, 88, **114**